Annabel Lee

Eternal Love & Melancholic Beauty
on the Edge of Sea and Memory

A Modern Translation
Adapted for the Contemporary Reader

Edgar Allan Poe

Translated by Tim Zengerink

Table of Contents

Preface
Message to the Reader

Rebuilding the Greatest Library in Human History

Thousands of years ago, the Library of Alexandria was the heart of global knowledge — a sanctuary where the wisdom of every known civilization was gathered and shared freely.

And then, it was lost.

Now, we're rebuilding it — and you are invited to join us.

At the Library of Alexandria, we've set out to make every book available to every person on Earth — not just in print, but in every language, every format, and for every reader.

Here's how we do it:

- **Deluxe Print Editions at True Printing Cost** - Order any book as a high-quality paperback, elegant hardcover, or stunning boxset — and only pay what it costs to print. No markups. No middlemen.
- **Unlimited Access to the Greatest Works** - Enjoy thousands of timeless classics — from Plato to Shakespeare to Tolstoy — in beautiful, modern eBook and audiobook editions. Read and listen without limits — for every reader, everywhere.
- **Modern Translations for Every Language & Dialect** - We're reimagining the classics in clear, accessible language — and translating them into every dialect imaginable. Everyone deserves to understand humanity's greatest ideas.

When you visit **LibraryofAlexandria.com**, you're not just accessing books — you're joining a global movement to restore, preserve, and share the wisdom of civilization.

Join us today at LibraryofAlexandria.com

Together, we'll ensure the light of human wisdom never fades again.

With gratitude,

The Modern Library of Alexandria Team

Visit:
www.libraryofalexandria.com
Or scan the code below:

Introduction

Poe's Final Ode to Love and Loss

Among Edgar Allan Poe's body of work, *Annabel Lee* stands as one of his most tender, lyrical, and haunting poems. First published in 1849, shortly after his untimely death, this poem is often regarded as a poetic farewell, a distillation of his recurring themes of love, death, memory, and the supernatural. While Poe is often associated with tales of terror and macabre imaginings, *Annabel Lee* showcases his ability to craft a narrative of love so pure and eternal that even death cannot sever its bonds. It is a poem that resonates with readers not only because of its musical beauty but also because of its deep emotional universality: the pain of loss and the enduring power of memory.

The narrative of *Annabel Lee* is both simple and profound. The poem tells the story of a young man who mourns his beloved *Annabel Lee*, a maiden "who lived with no other thought / than to love and be loved by me." Their love is described as so powerful and so pure that even the "winged seraphs of Heaven" become envious, leading to *Annabel Lee*'s untimely death. Yet, despite her passing, the speaker declares that their souls remain forever entwined, transcending the barriers of time and mortality. He continues to dream of her, to feel her presence, and to draw strength from the belief that their love is eternal.

Poe wrote *Annabel Lee* near the end of his life, and many readers and scholars have interpreted it as a tribute to his late wife, Virginia Clemm Poe, who died of tuberculosis at the age of 24. Virginia's early death left an indelible mark on

Poe's work, inspiring some of his most poignant meditations on the fragility of life and the enduring nature of love. In *Annabel Lee*, this personal grief is transformed into art, with Poe blending elements of fairy-tale romance, Gothic imagery, and lyrical repetition to create a poem that feels at once deeply personal and universally resonant.

The setting of the poem—a "kingdom by the sea"—is deliberately dreamlike and timeless. It evokes both the innocence of a childhood romance and the grandeur of a legendary love story. The sea, with its ceaseless ebb and flow, becomes a symbol of both constancy and change, reflecting the speaker's undying devotion as well as the inevitability of death. This interplay between the eternal and the ephemeral, the ideal and the tragic, is at the heart of *Annabel Lee*, making it one of Poe's most emotionally layered and enduring works.

Themes of Eternal Love, Loss, and Transcendence

One of the most powerful themes of *Annabel Lee* is the idea that true love transcends death. The speaker's devotion to *Annabel Lee* is not diminished by her physical absence; on the contrary, it is intensified by it. He believes that their love is stronger than the forces of nature, stronger even than the jealous angels who sought to separate them. This theme reflects both Poe's Romantic ideal of love as a spiritual and transcendent force and his personal longing for reunion with Virginia beyond the confines of mortal existence.

The poem also explores the theme of innocence and idealized love. *Annabel Lee* is described as a "maiden," suggesting a kind of pure, untainted affection that is untouched by the complexities or corruptions of the adult world. Their love is portrayed as both youthful and eternal, a union of souls rather than just bodies. This idealization of love is a hallmark of Poe's work, appearing in other poems such as *Eulalie*, *To One in Paradise*, and *Ulalume*, but it reaches its most poignant expression in *Annabel Lee*.

Loss and mourning form another crucial thread of the poem. While the speaker insists that death has not truly separated them, the tone of the poem is suffused with melancholy. The repetition of phrases like "in this kingdom by the sea" and "of the beautiful *Annabel Lee*" creates a hypnotic rhythm that mirrors the persistence of memory and the inability to move beyond grief. The poem becomes both a eulogy and a testament, a way for the speaker to keep *Annabel Lee* alive in his heart and in his words.

There is also a subtle undercurrent of rebellion in the poem. The speaker rejects the notion that death or divine will can end his love for *Annabel Lee*. By declaring that "neither the angels in Heaven above / nor the demons down under the sea / can ever dissever my soul from the soul / of the beautiful *Annabel Lee*," he asserts the supremacy of human passion over cosmic forces. This defiance reflects Poe's larger artistic vision, in which intense emotion often transcends or challenges the limits imposed by fate, time, and mortality.

The sea itself functions as a rich symbol throughout the poem. It represents both the eternal and the unknowable, a force that can separate lovers yet also unite them in memory and spirit. The imagery of the sea, the stars, and the moon all contribute to the poem's dreamlike quality, suggesting a connection between the earthly and the celestial, the finite and the infinite.

Poe's Style and
the Poem's Enduring Legacy

Poe's mastery of musicality is on full display in *Annabel Lee*. The poem's ballad-like structure, with its use of anapestic and iambic rhythms, creates a lilting, almost song-like quality that enhances its emotional impact. The repetition of key phrases—such as "kingdom by the sea" and "of the beautiful Annabel Lee"—serves both to reinforce the narrative and to create a sense of incantation, as though the speaker is chanting a spell to preserve his beloved's memory. This repetition, combined with the poem's rich use of alliteration and assonance, makes *Annabel Lee* one of Poe's most melodious and memorable works.

The language of the poem is simple yet evocative, blending the innocence of a fairy tale with the depth of a love elegy. Words like "maiden," "sepulchre," and "chilling" evoke both the beauty and the fragility of life, while the recurring references to the sea and the night sky suggest a love that is both earthly and eternal. The poem's final stanza, in which the speaker lies down beside *Annabel Lee*'s tomb by the sea, is both haunting and profoundly moving, encapsulating the fusion of love and death that defines much of Poe's work.

The cultural impact of *Annabel Lee* has been profound. It has been widely anthologized, memorized, and adapted in various forms of music, art, and film. Its themes of eternal love and tragic loss have resonated with generations of readers, making it one of Poe's most beloved poems. While it is often read as a personal expression of Poe's grief for Virginia, it also transcends its autobiographical origins, speaking to anyone who has experienced the pain of losing a loved one and the enduring power of memory.

For modern readers, *Annabel Lee* offers both a glimpse into the Romantic ideal of love and a timeless meditation on the human condition. It reminds us that love, at its deepest level, is not confined by time or space, but lives on in the mind, the heart, and the imagination. The poem's beauty lies not only in its language but also in its ability to evoke universal emotions of longing, devotion, and hope.

As you read *Annabel Lee*, consider the interplay of its themes and its form, the way Poe weaves together the imagery of the natural world with the emotions of the human heart. Notice how the repetition of sounds and phrases creates a sense of both comfort and obsession, mirroring the speaker's refusal to let go of his beloved. Through this delicate balance of music and meaning, Poe achieves a rare and enduring beauty, one that continues to captivate readers more than a century and a half after its creation.

Annabel Lee

It was many, many years ago, in a kingdom beside the sea, that a young woman lived there whom you might know by the name of *Annabel Lee*. This young woman lived with no other purpose than to love and be loved by me.

I was a child and she was a child, in this kingdom beside the sea, but we loved with a love that was more than love—Annabel Lee and I. We shared a love that the winged angels of heaven envied in her and me.

This was the reason that, long ago, in this kingdom beside the sea, a wind blew out of a cloud, making my beautiful Annabel Lee cold. Her noble relatives came and took her away from me, to lock her up in a tomb in this kingdom beside the sea.

The angels, not nearly as happy in heaven, became jealous of her and me. Yes, that was the reason, as everyone knows in this kingdom beside the sea, that the wind came out of the cloud at night, chilling and killing my Annabel Lee.

But our love was much stronger than the love of those who were older than us, of many who were much wiser than us. Neither the angels in heaven above nor the demons down under the sea can ever separate my soul from the soul of the beautiful Annabel Lee.

The moon never shines without bringing me dreams of the beautiful Annabel Lee. The stars never rise without me seeing the bright eyes of the beautiful Annabel Lee. So, all through the night, I lie down beside my darling, my darling, my life and my bride, in her tomb there by the sea, in her grave by the side of the sea.

A Valentine

For her this poem is written, whose bright eyes,
Brilliantly expressive like the twins of Leda,
Will discover her own sweet name, which lies nestled
Upon the page, hidden from every reader.
Look carefully through the lines!
—they contain a treasure
Divine—a charm—a protective token
That must be carried close to the heart.
Examine closely the rhythm—
The words—the syllables! Do not overlook
The smallest detail, or you might waste your effort!
And yet there exists in this no impossible puzzle
Which one could not solve without a sword,
If one could simply understand the scheme.
Written upon the page where now are gazing
Eyes sparkling with soul, there lie hidden
Three eloquent words often spoken in the presence
Of poets by poets—as the name belongs to a poet, too.
Its letters, though naturally positioned
Like the knight Pinto—Mendez Ferdinando—
Still create a word meaning Truth—Stop attempting!
You will not solve the mystery,
no matter how hard you try.

An Enigma

"We rarely discover," declares Solomon Don Dunce, "even half a meaningful thought in the most profound sonnet. We can see right through all these flimsy creations just as easily as we can see through a delicate Naples bonnet—complete rubbish of the worst kind!—how can any woman possibly wear such a thing? Yet these poems are far more burdensome than your typical Petrarchan verse—soft, meaningless nonsense that the slightest breeze can twist into wrapping paper while you're still trying to study it." And truly, Solomon speaks the truth. The typical poetic pretensions are nothing but sheer nonsense—fleeting and so see-through—but this particular work is different—you can count on it—solid, substantial, eternal—all because of the precious names that are hidden within it.

To My Mother

Because I believe that in the heavens above, the angels, whispering to one another, can find, among their passionate words of love, none so sacred as the word "Mother," therefore by that precious name I have long called you— you who are more than a mother to me, and fill my deepest heart, where Death placed you when it set my Virginia's spirit free. My mother—my own mother, who died young, was only the mother of myself; but you are mother to the one I loved so deeply, and thus you are more precious than the mother I knew by that same infinite measure by which my wife was more precious to my soul than life itself.

For Annie

Thank Heaven! the crisis—
The danger has passed,
And the lingering illness
Has ended at last—
And the fever called "Living"
Has been conquered at last.

Sadly, I know,
I have lost all my strength,
And no muscle I move
As I lie at full length—
But no matter!—I feel
I am better at length.

And I rest so peacefully,
Now in my bed,
That any observer
Might think me dead—
Might be startled at seeing me
Believing me dead.

The moaning and groaning,
The sighing and sobbing,
Have quieted now,
With that horrible throbbing
At heart:—ah, that horrible,
Horrible throbbing!

The sickness—the nausea—
The merciless pain—
Have stopped, with the fever
That drove my brain mad—
With the fever called "Living"
That burned in my brain.

And oh! of all tortures
That torture the worst
Has lessened—the terrible
Torture of thirst,
For the naphthaline river
Of Passion accursed:—
I have drunk of a water
That quenches all thirst:—

Of a water that flows,
With a lullaby sound,
From a spring but a very few
Feet under ground—
From a cavern not very far
Down under ground.

And ah! let it never
Be foolishly said
That my room is gloomy
And narrow my bed—
For man never slept
In a different bed;
And, to sleep, you must slumber
In just such a bed.

My tormented spirit
Here peacefully rests,
Forgetting, or never
Regretting its roses—
Its old agitations
Of myrtles and roses:

For now, while so quietly
Lying, it imagines
A holier fragrance
About it, of pansies—
A rosemary fragrance,
Mixed with pansies—
With rue and the beautiful
Puritan pansies.

And so it lies happily,
Bathing in many
A dream of the truth
And the beauty of Annie—
Drowned in a bath
Of the hair of Annie.

She tenderly kissed me,
She lovingly caressed,
And then I fell gently
To sleep on her breast—
Deeply to sleep
From the heaven of her breast.

When the light was put out,
She covered me warmly,
And she prayed to the angels

To keep me from harm—
To the queen of the angels
To shield me from harm.

And I lie so peacefully,
Now in my bed
(Knowing her love)
That you think me dead—
And I rest so contentedly,
Now in my bed,
(With her love at my breast)
That you think me dead—
That you shudder to look at me,
Believing me dead.

But my heart is brighter
Than all of the many
Stars in the sky,
For it sparkles with Annie—
It glows with the light
Of the love of my Annie—
With the thought of the light
Of the eyes of my Annie.

To F——

Beloved! amid the sincere sorrows
That gather around my earthly journey—
(Bleak journey, unfortunately! where grows
Not even one solitary rose)—
My soul at least finds comfort
In dreams of you, and in them discovers
A paradise of gentle peace.

And so your memory is to me
Like some magical distant island
In some turbulent sea—
Some ocean pulsing far and wild
With tempest—but where meanwhile
Most peaceful skies continuously
Just over that one bright land smile.

To Frances S. Osgood

You want to be loved? Then don't let your heart stray from its current path. Continue being everything you are right now, and don't become anything you're not. When you interact with the world this way, your gentle manner, your grace, and your beauty that goes beyond the physical will become an endless source of praise. And love will become a simple duty.

Eldorado

Dressed in bright colors,
A brave knight,
In sunlight and in darkness,
Had traveled far,
Singing a song,
Looking for Eldorado.
But he became old—
This knight so brave—
And across his heart a darkness
Fell as he discovered
No piece of land
That resembled Eldorado.

And, as his power
Left him finally,
He encountered a wandering shadow—
"Shadow," he said,
"Where might it be—
This land of Eldorado?"

"Beyond the Mountains
Of the Moon,
Down the Valley of the Shadow,
Travel, bravely travel,"
The spirit answered,
"If you search for Eldorado!"

Eulalie

I dwelt alone
In a world of moan,
And my soul was a stagnant tide,
Till the fair and gentle Eulalie
became my blushing bride—
Till the yellow-haired young Eulalie
became my smiling bride.
Ah, less—less bright
The stars of the night
Than the eyes of the radiant girl!
And never a flake
That the vapor can make
With the moon-tints of purple and pearl,
Can vie with the modest Eulalie's
most unregarded curl—
Can compare with the bright-eyed
Eulalie's most humble and careless curl.
Now Doubt—now Pain
Come never again,
For her soul gives me sigh for sigh,
And all day long
Shines, bright and strong,
Astarté within the sky,
While ever to her dear Eulalie
upturns her matron eye—
While ever to her young Eulalie
upturns her violet eye.

A Dream within a Dream

Take this kiss upon your forehead! And as I leave you now, let me admit this much—you're not mistaken when you believe that my life has been nothing but a dream. But even if hope has disappeared in a single night, or in just one day, whether in a vision or without one, does that make it any less lost? Everything we observe or appear to be is simply a dream inside another dream.

I stand surrounded by the thundering sound of waves crashing against a tormented shoreline, and I clutch grains of golden sand in my hand—so few of them! Yet watch how they slip through my fingers into the depths while I cry— while I cry! Oh God! Can't I hold them with a firmer grip? Oh God! Can't I rescue even one grain from the merciless wave? Is everything we observe or appear to be nothing more than a dream within a dream?

Marie Louise (Shew)

Of everyone who welcomes your presence like the dawn—
of everyone for whom your absence feels like night—the
complete erasure from the heavens above of the sacred
sun—of everyone who, through tears, blesses you every
hour for hope—for life—and most of all, for bringing back
to life the deeply buried faith in truth, in virtue, in
humanity—of everyone who, lying down to die on despair's
unholy bed, has suddenly risen at your gently whispered
words, "Let there be light!" At your gently whispered words
that came true in the angelic gleaming of your eyes—of
everyone who owes you the most, whose gratitude most
closely resembles worship—oh, remember the most faithful,
the most passionately devoted, and know that these humble
lines are written by him—by him who, as he writes them,
trembles to think his soul is connecting with an angel's.

To Marie Louise (Shew)

Not long ago, the person writing these words, in the wild arrogance of intellectual thinking, insisted on "the power of words"—argued that never could a thought emerge within the human mind beyond what the human tongue could express: And now, as if mocking that claim, two words— two foreign gentle syllables—Italian sounds, created only to be whispered by angels dreaming in the moonlit "dew that hangs like chains of pearl on Hermon hill,"—have awakened from the depths of his heart, thoughts beyond thought that are the essence of thinking, richer, far more untamed, far more divine visions than even the seraph musician, Israfel, (who has "the sweetest voice of all God's creatures,") could hope to speak. And I! my magic is shattered. The pen drops helpless from my trembling hand. With your precious name as my subject, though concealed by you, I cannot write—I cannot speak or think—sadly, I cannot feel; for this is not feeling, this standing still upon the golden doorway of the wide-open entrance of dreams, staring, mesmerized, down the magnificent view, and trembling as I see, on the right, on the left, and all along the path, among purple-tinted mists, far away to where the scene ends—only you!

The City in the Sea

Look! Death has built himself a throne in a strange city that lies alone, far down in the dim West, where the good and the bad and the worst and the best have gone to their eternal rest. There, shrines and palaces and towers (time-worn towers that do not tremble!) look like nothing we know. All around, forgotten by the lifting winds, the melancholy waters lie resignedly beneath the sky.

No rays from holy Heaven shine down on the long night-time of that town; but light from the eerie sea streams up the towers silently—gleams up the tall spires far and free—up domes—up spires—up royal halls—up temples—up walls like those of Babylon—up shadowy long-forgotten gardens of carved ivy and stone flowers—up many and many a marvelous shrine whose twisted decorative bands weave together the musical instrument, the violet, and the vine.

Resignedly beneath the sky the melancholy waters lie. The towers and shadows blend together there so much that everything seems to hang suspended in air, while from a proud tower in the town Death looks down with gigantic presence.

There, open temples and gaping graves stretch level with the glowing waves; but not the riches that lie there in each statue's diamond eye—not the brightly jeweled dead tempt the waters from their resting place; for no ripples curl, sadly! along that wilderness of glass—no swellings show that winds might exist on some distant happier sea—no movements suggest that winds have blown on seas less terrifyingly calm.

But look, there is a stirring in the air! The wave—there is movement there! As if the towers had pushed aside, while slightly sinking, the dull tide—as if their tops had weakly created an empty space within the hazy Heaven. The waves now have a redder glow—the hours are breathing faint and low—and when, without any earthly groans, down, down that town shall sink away, Hell, rising from a thousand thrones, shall honor it with reverence.

THE END

Thank You For Reading

You've Just Read a Piece of the Greatest Library Ever Rebuilt

Thank you for reading.

This book is one of thousands we're restoring, reimagining, and translating as part of the **Modern Library of Alexandria** — a global movement to preserve and share humanity's most important ideas.

What was once lost to fire and time is now rising again — not just as memory, but as living, breathing knowledge, freely accessible to all.

What You Can Do Next:

- **Keep Reading.**

  Discover more legendary works — in beautiful print, audiobook, or digital form — at LibraryofAlexandria.com.

- **Build Your Own Library.**

  Every title is available as a paperback, hardcover, or collectible boxset — at true printing cost. Craft a personal library worthy of display.

- **Spread the Light.**

  Share this book. Tell others about the movement. Help us translate every timeless work into every language, so no reader is ever left behind.

By finishing this book, you've already taken part in something extraordinary.

Join us at LibraryofAlexandria.com

Together, we're rebuilding the greatest library the world has ever known.

With appreciation,

The Modern Library of Alexandria Team

Visit:
www.libraryofalexandria.com
Or scan the code below: